Witch's
HERBAL PRIMER

A BEGINNER'S GUIDE TO PLANT MAGIC

AMY CESARI

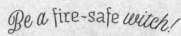

Be a fire-safe witch!

Lots of space above
and around the flame.

Candle is on a
fire-safe dish.

Never leave
flames unattended.

THIS BOOK BELONGS TO:

....

HERBAL MAGIC

You may feel innately called to "know" plants. Perhaps you're sensitive to their shapes, smells, and tastes, or you've wanted to learn more about them for as long as you can remember.

This desire to know plants is wired into our bodies and collective consciousness. Plants were our first sources of food and medicine, and we relied on what we could forage and grow for survival.

Studying plants magically or medicinally is ancient, innate in you, and yours to explore.

The plant world is a source of life-energy and divine power, also known as "natural magic."

Natural magic is a practice of channeling the creative power of the earth within yourself and into your circle of magic and sphere of influence.

If you seek the wisdom of nature with a genuine intention, nature will reward you with the magic, secrets, and mysteries that you're looking for.

YOUR HERBAL JOURNEY

This book is a canvas to explore the world of plants and herbs through your own experiences.

An "herbal" is a book that features practical remedies, recipes, or rituals that use the power of plants. Herbals are often more anecdotal than scientific, skimming over the factual intricacies of how things work.

Ancient herbals often contained information passed down from older works as well as first-hand accounts, and this book was created in the same spirit. There's a collection of herbal information common to the modern witch, but more important—it has space for you to add what you've learned about working with herbs in your own practice.

Follow your intuition on your own herbal journey, as you learn about plants in a way that suits your life and study.

This book does not attempt—in any way—to cover the many ancient histories of herbalism. There is much more to explore when it comes to the study of plants, and it is woven deeply into cultural traditions of food, medicine, and ritual.

SOME HELPFUL TIPS

LESS IS MORE: You don't have to know "everything." You can get acquainted with one herb at a time. And it's okay if you work with a handful of herbs—even just a couple to begin.

PATIENCE: A journey of magic or a deep study like herbalism is eternally unfolding. There is no destination or "end." You will glean wisdom with time, so take that time and make it magical, educational, and meaningful to you.

The things you don't know yet are your potential, not your lack of knowledge. Consider working at an unhurried pace when learning something new, and give yourself time and space to let the magic unfold.

WHAT TO WRITE is entirely up to you. But here are some tips and ideas to get you started.

- Anything useful or interesting about plants.
- Magical uses of plants.
- A record of how you've used herbs in ritual.
- Medicinal knowledge or things you've learned about how plants can help your body.
- Recipes and culinary uses of herbs.
- A record of herbs you've grown or of plants

you've seen in the wilderness.

- Herbs that are indigenous to where you live or to another place of significance.

- Herbs that are used to honor your gods, your higher power, or your personal body and self.

SAFETY & PRECAUTIONS:

POISON: *THIS IS WITCHCRAFT, AND THERE WILL BE POISON!* Since this is primarily a book of herbs famed by witches, many of the herbs listed are poisonous and not intended for consumption. It's advisable to use these poisons symbolically. If you do choose to work with poisonous plants in person—do so at your own risk.

MEDICINAL HERBS: This book is for entertainment purposes only and is NOT intended to be a medicinal herb book in any way. A few common medicinal uses (like herbal teas) are listed for informational purposes. However, do not take anything in this book as medical health advice, and ALWAYS research and ask your herbalist or healthcare provider before ingesting even the most basic herbs, especially if you are pregnant, breastfeeding, or have health-related concerns.

ETHICS OF FORAGING: The easiest rule is, don't forage or pick things without explicit permission. Grow your own herbs or buy them ethically instead.

If you choose to forage, become overly researched about what is legal in your area. Know which plants are protected, endangered, or otherwise not okay to take.

Do your due diligence about legalities and trespassing laws.

And if you have any doubt over whether something is suitable to pick when foraging — don't take the chance.

MOST OF ALL... HAVE FUN!

While there's nothing inherently "safe" about wielding the powers of herbal magic and witchcraft, it certainly is a lot of fun. Follow your spirit, and revel in every bit of magic that you discover along the way.

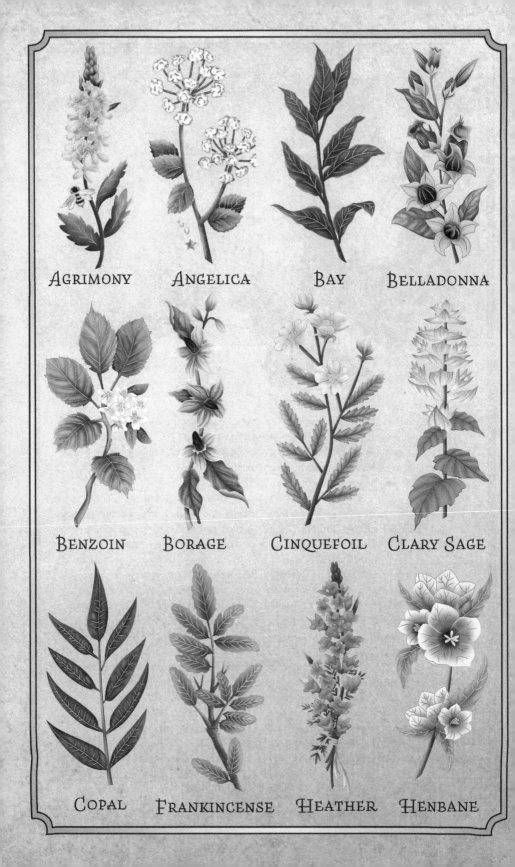

AGRIMONY ANGELICA BAY BELLADONNA

BENZOIN BORAGE CINQUEFOIL CLARY SAGE

COPAL FRANKINCENSE HEATHER HENBANE

- Cypress -
Life, Death, &
Immortality

- Sage -
Wisdom &
Protection

- Yarrow -
Hex Breaking &
Spiritual Strength

- Mugwort -
Visions

- Oak -
Magic & Strength

- Elderflower -
Protection & Magic

- Agrimony -
Protection &
Witch Power

- Bay -
Prophecy, Strength, &
Purification

RITUAL HERBS

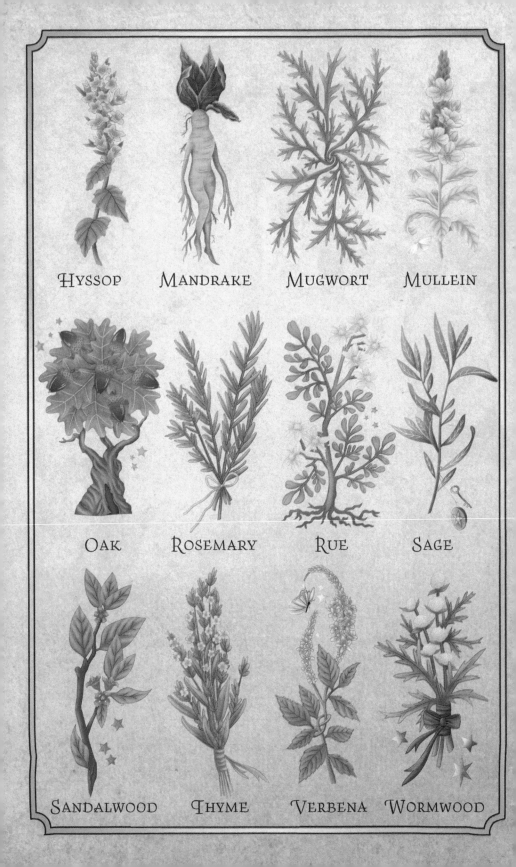

HYSSOP MANDRAKE MUGWORT MULLEIN

OAK ROSEMARY RUE SAGE

SANDALWOOD THYME VERBENA WORMWOOD

THE POWER OF PLANTS

Use the magic of herbs with your own personal or divine power to create change and growth.

PLANT SPIRITS & HERBAL MAGIC:

Many believe that plants have spirits and even souls and psyches. Experiencing nature through awe-inspiring scenery, plants, and animals can reconnect you to your spirit and source of magic.

Ancient cultures used herbs in their rituals for these same reasons. Plant magic is powerful, as it is a channeling of divinity and the energy of the earth.

PREPARING HERBS FOR RITUAL:

Some witches consecrate their herbs before ritual use with a simple spell or two, such as:
- Place ritual herbs under the full moon.
- Wash herbs in spring or salt water.
- Set herbs within a pentacle of burning candles.
- Harvest herbs with intention for ritual use.

Most importantly, set the intention (feel the feeling) of what you want to manifest as you perform any of these preparatory rites.

WAYS TO USE HERBS IN RITUAL

There are infinite ways to work with herbs in your spells and rituals. *If you're new to spellcasting, make sure to read the beginner's instructions in the back of this book.*

ELEMENTAL MAGIC: Elementals are a simple yet effective way to cast spells with herbs. Try these powerful elemental mechanisms, and check out the *Herbs & the Elements* index page in the back of this book for more information:

AIR: Toss herbs to the wind or feed birds.

EARTH: Tend to the earth and plant seeds.

FIRE: Cast herbs into a fire, burn incense, or anoint candles with oil and crushed herbs.

WATER: Pass herbal sprigs through a running body of water or ocean waves.

DEITIES AND SPIRITS: Spiritual practitioners often use herbs to venerate or call upon deities and earth spirits. These rituals can be simple, like placing herbs on your altar or giving an offering.

SPELLS AND CHARMS: Witches use herbs and plants to create containers of magic, such as:
- Charm bags, bottles, and poppets (dolls).
- Kitchen and culinary spells, or food as ritual.
- Oils, tinctures, soaps, baths, candles, potions, and "things" made with herbal ingredients.
- Wreaths, crowns, garlands, and bouquets.

And of course, the witch's garden brings all manner of magic to life.

RITUALS OF GROWING AND HARVESTING:

Become intimately involved with dirt and plants. Go deeper by planting and harvesting by the phases of the moon or by the Witch's Sabbats.

TOOLS FOR MAGICAL HERBALISM:

The most important part of herbal magic—other than the plants—is your inner power. Know what you want from your spell and hold to that feeling as if it already exists.

HERBS: Procure your plants in the most ethical and magical ways that you can, and store them in an organized and sacred manner.

TOOLS: Use sharp scissors or shears to cut herbs. A mortar and pestle is useful but not always necessary. Beyond that, you may not need additional tools, but here are some suggestions:

AN ALTAR is nice to have, but not essential.

INCENSE requires a good censer or cauldron, matches, and sometimes, quality charcoal.

CANDLES should be made of beeswax or a natural wax, and have a safe place to burn them.

And... always write down notes about your magical work and experiences. Use this book and additional notebooks and sources of information to keep your magic moving forward.

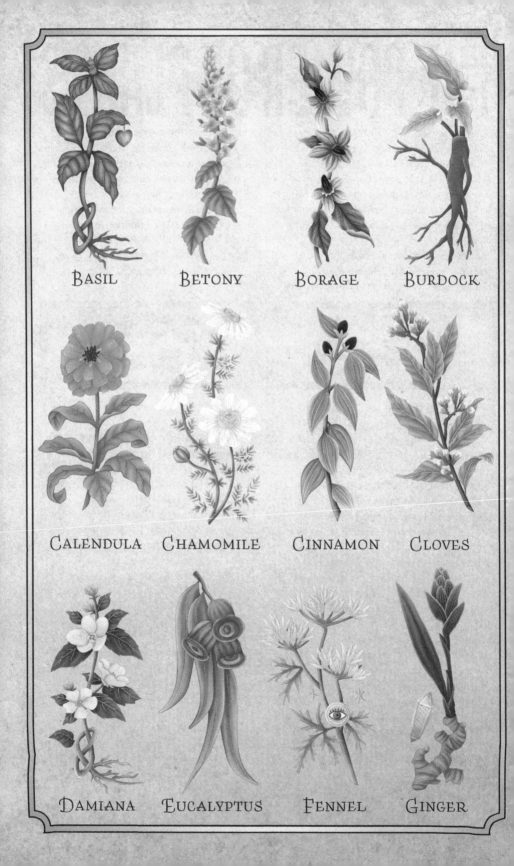

BASIL BETONY BORAGE BURDOCK

CALENDULA CHAMOMILE CINNAMON CLOVES

DAMIANA EUCALYPTUS FENNEL GINGER

MEDICINAL HERBS

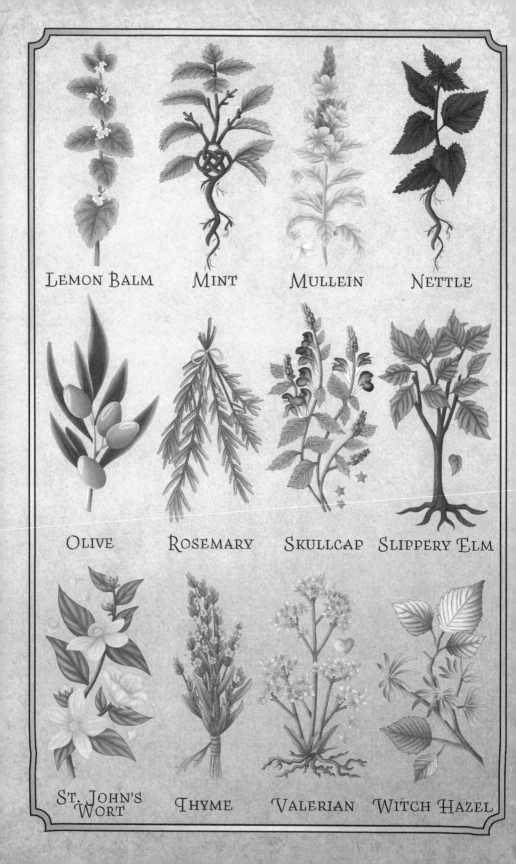

LEMON BALM   MINT   MULLEIN   NETTLE

OLIVE   ROSEMARY   SKULLCAP   SLIPPERY ELM

ST. JOHN'S WORT   THYME   VALERIAN   WITCH HAZEL

THE POWER OF HEALTH

Explore the paths and traditions of medicinal herbalism if you want to learn how herbs can help the human body and mind.

While medicinals are obviously not the focus of this book, a few extremely common teas and usages are listed. If you have any serious health concerns, reach out to herbal practitioners as well as your modern healthcare provider.

COMMON PRACTICAL HERBAL REMEDIES:

Shop around in the herbal tea section of your grocery, and you'll find ancient remedies for the digestive, circulatory, immune, nervous, and respiratory systems, as well as topical herbs for fighting infection and helping to manage disorders of the skin. There are hundreds of relatively safe, legal herbs that you can try right away. Always double-check if you are pregnant, breastfeeding, or have health concerns.

MEDICINAL HISTORIES: Before the evolution of modern medicine, people healed themselves with what they could find and grow—mostly plants. Thousands of plants have powerful medicinal properties, and diverse herbal medicinal traditions evolved in cultures worldwide.

The majority of "modern" medicines are still made with plants and their derivatives. Traditional herbal medicinals are having a resurgence in popularity in many modern cultures, as people reawaken to methods and practices that have been in use for thousands of years.

HOW HERBS WORK AS MEDICINE

The natural chemicals in herbs can affect the systems of the body, and when used wisely, can promote good health and healing. Each plant contains a different and complex combination of constituents, and they interact with the systems of the human body in their own unique ways.

FURTHER STUDY: If this subject calls to you, follow your curiosity. Start reading, learning, and practicing. There are many valuable and well-researched books and courses available on medicinal herbs—waiting for you to find them.

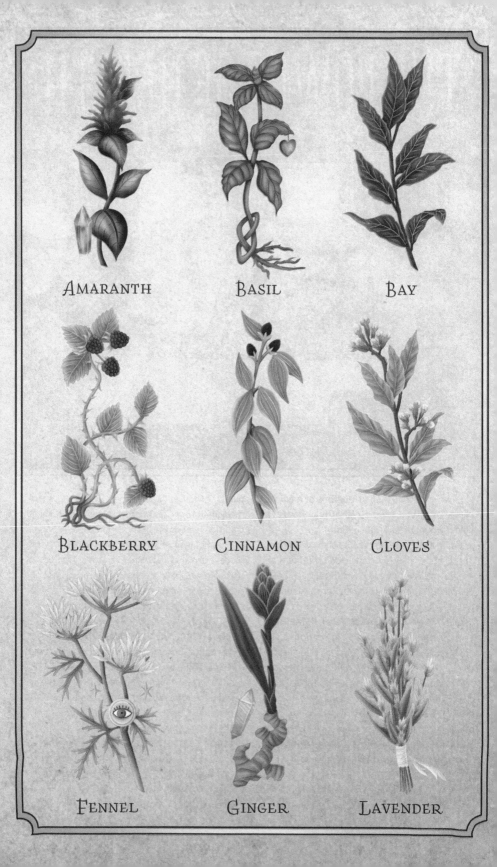

AMARANTH   BASIL   BAY

BLACKBERRY   CINNAMON   CLOVES

FENNEL   GINGER   LAVENDER

CULINARY HERBS

AND KITCHEN WITCHCRAFT

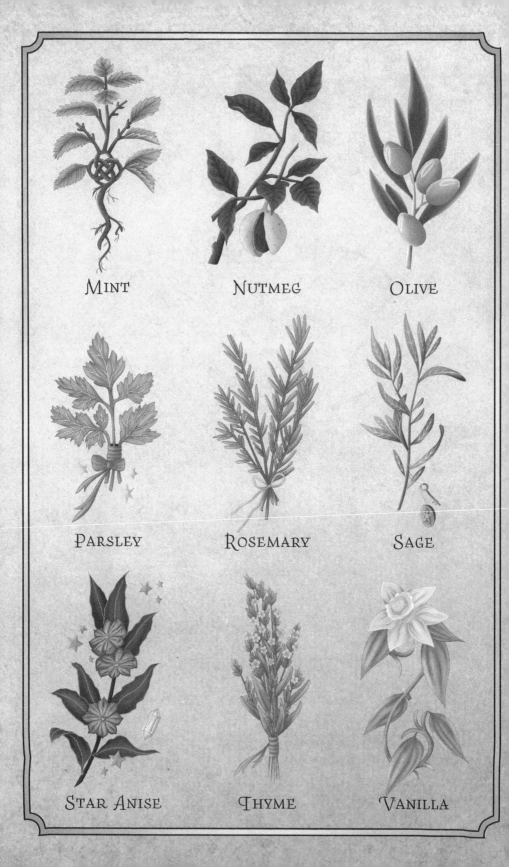

MINT

NUTMEG

OLIVE

PARSLEY

ROSEMARY

SAGE

STAR ANISE

THYME

VANILLA

THE POWER OF FOOD

If you want to enhance your life with practical, nourishing spellwork, you can explore the world of culinary herbs and kitchen witchcraft.

Kitchen herbs blur the lines between food, medicine, and everyday magic. In many traditional cultures, ancient people placed deities and ancestry at the center of the hearth or cooking place—aligning these powerful forces with the everyday processes of sustaining life.

The kitchen, hearth, and cauldron all convey deep symbolism of life, death, and the natural magic of herbs and plants. With the act of cooking, raw ingredients become something entirely new and valuable. Cooking is a sacred, yet everyday form of transmutation, manipulation, and magic.

Kitchen witchcraft and "everyday" magic is as simple as blessing your food, eating certain herbs for magical purposes, preparing food with intention, or cooking in honor of a deity, an ancestor, or a seasonal celebration.

Seek out herbs that match the magical and culinary properties (and medicinal, for bonus points) that you desire, and explore new flavors, preparations, and culinary experiences to keep your kitchen witchcraft fresh.

MATERIA MAGICKA

ACONITE

"WOLFSBANE"

PLANET: SATURN. ELEMENT: WATER.

POISON: Virulently poisonous. Do not take internally or touch with your bare skin. This herb is best used symbolically, viewed in the wild, or substituted with dark purple candles or a nontoxic purple flower.

FOLKLORE: A legendary baneful herb and infamous herbal poison, aconite protects humans against vampires and werewolves. Aconite can transport you to the spirit world (literally) and is a common ingredient in medieval witches' flying potions.

The Greek goddess Hekate discovered aconite in the slobber of Cerberus, the three-headed dog at the gates of Hell. Aconite also has shapeshifting and transformational properties, as Athena used the herb to turn Arachne into a spider.

GARDEN: If you grow aconite to honor the goddess Hekate, use extreme caution. Always wear gloves when handling it, and keep it away from pets and children.

SPELLCRAFT: Use the symbol of aconite and a witch's broom to fly beyond the limitations of society and your self-imposed boundaries.

AMARANTH

PLANET: SUN or SATURN. ELEMENT: FIRE.

MAGICAL PROPERTIES: Immortality of the soul. Spiritual powers and healing. Sacred to the Aztec sun god Huitzilopochtli, and an offering to Artemis and Demeter in Greek lore.

KITCHEN: A staple food for Aztec people, grind toasted amaranth seeds to make tortillas, or sweeten them with honey to make candy.

RITUALS: Use amaranth flowers to decorate graves, tombs, and altars to deities.

SPELLCRAFT: Wear a crown of amaranth for energetic invisibility and spiritual healing. Amaranth flowers can be crushed into a natural red dye and cosmetic pigment.

Mend your broken heart with a bouquet of dried roses and amaranth flowers.

AGRIMONY

PLANET: JUPITER. ELEMENT: AIR.

MAGICAL PROPERTIES: Counter-magic and energetic protection. Promotes sleep. Protects against goblins, spirits, and unwanted energy.

MEDICINAL PROPERTIES: Bitter and astringent, use agrimony as a tonic for the stomach or skin.

BATH: Draw a bath with agrimony and mugwort leaves to heal your spirit and promote sleep.

KITCHEN: Drink agrimony tea with lemon for upset stomach, cough, or sore throat.

SABBATS: Protect yourself from goblins on Samhain with a wreath or crown of agrimony.

SPELLCRAFT: Place agrimony under your pillow or make a sachet with lavender for restful sleep. For counter-magical protection, mix agrimony with salt and sprinkle it around your home.

ANGELICA

PLANET: SUN. ELEMENT: FIRE.

MAGICAL PROPERTIES: Energetic and spiritual protection. Hex breaking.

MEDICINAL PROPERTIES: Warming yet bitter, angelica root tea can help relieve coughs, indigestion, and achy joints. Do not ingest while pregnant.

BATH: Add angelica root and sea salt to your bath for spiritual cleansing and to neutralize the influence of others.

HOME: Grow angelica around your house for energetic protection. Burn angelica as incense to bless your home.

KITCHEN: The bitter angelica root can be candied for a sweet treat.

SPELLCRAFT: To protect your energy when you leave the house, carry angelica in a white charm bag or cloth.

BASIL
"THE WITCH'S HERB"
PLANET: MARS. ELEMENT: FIRE.

MAGICAL PROPERTIES: Love and wealth. Creating harmony and cleansing energetic spaces. An ingredient in flying potions.

MEDICINAL PROPERTIES: A mild sedative. Soothes digestion, anxiety, and skin irritations.

BATH: A hot bath with basil leaves will strengthen your aura. Anoint your chakras with basil oil to balance your energy.

GARDEN: Grow basil for protection and wealth. Harvest basil on the summer solstice to imbue it with magic.

HOME: Burn basil as incense or use in a floor wash to purify the energy of your space.

KITCHEN: Cook with basil to encourage peaceful relationships. De-stress with basil tea, pesto, or by sniffing fresh basil leaves.

SPELLCRAFT: For courage, carry a sachet of basil or rub basil oil on your shoes. Eat basil to counteract the fear of growth, change, and the unknown.

BAY

PLANET: SUN. ELEMENT: FIRE.

MAGICAL PROPERTIES: Prophecy, vision, strength, healing, and purification.

MEDICINAL PROPERTIES: Eases aches and promotes digestion.

RITUAL: An essential herb in Greek and Roman ritual practices. Use a bay sprig as a wand to sprinkle blessed water or moon water. A crown of bay will purify and protect your spirit. Burn bay leaves as a visioning incense. Decorate with and burn bay for Saturnalia, Yule, and Imbolc.

KITCHEN: Bay leaves add strength and purification to your witch's stew. Create a flavorful charm by bundling bay leaves with cloves of garlic, parsley, and thyme.

BATH: Add a decoction of bay to your bath to relieve your spirit and muscles.

SPELLCRAFT: Carry an amulet of bay for protection. Predict an outcome by burning a bay leaf. A leaf that crackles is a favorable omen.

ONYX
Carries a similar magic to Belladonna

IRON
Consecrate iron tools with the energy of Belladonna

BELLADONNA
"DEADLY NIGHTSHADE"
PLANET: SATURN. ELEMENT: WATER.

POISON: Virulently poisonous. Do not take internally or touch. Use symbolically or substitute with nontoxic candles, berries, or flowers in dark purple, red, or black.

MAGICAL PROPERTIES: Vision, astral projection, and death. An essential herb for flying potion. Sacred to dark goddesses such as Atropos, Hekate, Circe, and Bellona.

RITUALS: Harvest only on Walpurgis night after releasing a black hen so the devil doesn't catch you in his garden.

BETONY
"WOOD BETONY"

PLANET: JUPITER. ELEMENT: FIRE.

MAGICAL PROPERTIES: An ancient cure-all for nearly every illness, as well as the banishment of all evil.

MEDICINAL PROPERTIES: Relieves headache and sinus pressure.

GARDEN: Grow wood betony as a protective plant around your home. Gather the flowers and sprinkle them on your doorsteps and windowsills.

SABBATS: Burn a pyre of betony on midsummer and jump through the smoke to purify your body and spirit.

SELF-CARE: Drink a tea of betony, comfrey, and lime flowers to relieve sinus pressure. Place wood betony leaves on your pillow to ward off nightmares.

BENZOIN

PLANET: SUN. ELEMENT: AIR.

MAGICAL PROPERTIES: A powerful ritual herb. Benzoin promotes concentration, focus, spiritual journey, meditation, and inner peace. The resin lends power and luck for success in spell casting and magical endeavors.

MEDICINAL PROPERTIES: Benzoin disinfects skin and relieves minor irritations. The scent of the oil can relieve respiratory congestion.

RITUALS: Burn benzoin incense to bring about an air of spiritual focus or harmony and emotional balance.

BATH: Add two drops of (stryax) benzoin oil and a handful of Epsom salt to a hot bath to relieve a cough or cold.

Betony soothes frayed nerves.

BLACKBERRY

PLANET: VENUS. ELEMENT: WATER

MAGICAL PROPERTIES: Protection, health, and prosperity. Sacred to ancient European witches and the goddess Brigid as it sustains life with its fruit and protects with its brambles.

MEDICINAL PROPERTIES: The fruit contains powerful anti-inflammatory and antioxidant properties. The leaves are astringent and make a lovely gargle for a sore throat.

RITUALS: Crawl under a bramble arch backwards to protect yourself from ills.

SABBATS: Bake a blackberry pie on Lughnasadh to celebrate the sacrifice of the harvest.

BIRCH

PLANET: VENUS. ELEMENT: WATER.

MAGICAL PROPERTIES: Protection, purification, and light. The energy of the divine feminine. A sacred tree.

MEDICINAL PROPERTIES: Birch provides anti-inflammatory relief for minor aches, pains, and swelling.

FOLKLORE: If Thor strikes a birch tree with lightning, its bark will have extra power as a magical parchment.

RITUALS: Make a witch's broom with a birch handle. A birch twig wand will consecrate new things. Sit in a birch grove to commune with Mother Earth. Birch bark will stoke your cauldron flame.

SABBATS: Make protective wreaths or otherwise decorate with birch twigs at Imbolc, Beltane, and Midsummer.

BLACKTHORN

PLANET: MARS.   ELEMENT: FIRE.

MAGICAL PROPERTIES: A symbol of the dark half of the year. Blackthorn represents witch power, protection, and manifesting wishes. Sacred to the crone or dark goddess Cailleach.

MEDICINAL PROPERTIES: Anti-inflammatory, astringent, and stimulating.

FOLKLORE: A witch's tree, known as "Crone of the Woods." Blackthorn's berries, called "sloe berries," were a staple food in some ancient European diets. Blackthorn is the darkest of the three sacred faeries' trees (Blackthorn, Hawthorn, and Rowan).

GARDEN: Don't cut down an enchanted blackthorn tree. Its guardian faeries will retaliate.

SABBATS: Burn blackthorn on Beltane to purify your spirit and cast away the darkness. Make sloe berry jam for a Samhain treat. Ferment your sloe gin for the months between Mabon and Yule.

SPELLCRAFT: Hang a blackthorn charm over your doorway to ward off undue influences and spirits. Blackthorn makes an excellent wand wood.

BORAGE

PLANET: JUPITER. ELEMENT: AIR.

MAGICAL PROPERTIES: Courage in crisis, protection, and psychic powers. Fortifying the power of your inner self and generating feelings of happiness from within.

MEDICINAL PROPERTIES: Soothes respiratory issues, inflamed skin, and stress.

SELF-CARE: Drink borage tea or take a bath with borage leaves and flowers to replenish your spirit and reconnect to your intuition.

BURDOCK

PLANET: VENUS. ELEMENT: WATER.

MAGICAL PROPERTIES: Protection and health.

MEDICINAL PROPERTIES: Detoxifying, antiseptic, and anti-inflammatory. Combine burdock root and dandelion root in a decoction to ease skin conditions.

SELF-CARE: Drink burdock tea to detoxify body and spirit.

SPELLCRAFT: Gather burdock root on the waning moon. Dry the roots for several months, then cut them into small pieces. String them on a thread, like beads. Wear or hang the beaded string for a delightfully witchy protection charm.

CALENDULA

PLANET: SUN. ELEMENT: FIRE.

MAGICAL PROPERTIES: Protection, psychic powers, and uplifting spirits. A popular herb for divination teas, séances, and spirit work.

MEDICINAL PROPERTIES: Astringent, anti-inflammatory, detoxifying, and antimicrobial.

KITCHEN: Dry calendula petals and put them in soups, salads, vinegars, rice dishes, and sandwiches to imbue your cooking with bright spiritual energy.

SABBATS: For the strongest magical qualities, harvest on the summer solstice at noon.

SELF-CARE: Craft a spiritually cleansing black soap with activated charcoal, calendula, rose, chamomile, tea tree oil, rosemary, and sage.

Stir your chamomile tea counterclockwise and imagine a peaceful night's sleep.

CHAMOMILE

PLANET: SUN.   ELEMENT: WATER.

MAGICAL PROPERTIES: Counter-magic, protection, peace, and love. Egyptian and European varieties have been used in ritual and medicine for thousands of years.

MEDICINAL PROPERTIES: Used as a sedative and reliever of headache, digestive upset, and minor skin inflammation. Anti-septic and anti-inflammatory.

BATH: Take a bath with chamomile and lavender to clear your energy and attract love.

HOME & GARDEN: Grow along walkways for a peaceful aromatic. Strew the flowers or keep a cauldron of dried flowers for a pleasant energy and aromatic presence.

SPELLCRAFT: Remove spells, hexes, and vibes cast in your direction by sprinkling chamomile flowers around your house or at the doors and windows.

CINQUEFOIL

PLANET: JUPITER. ELEMENT: FIRE.

MAGICAL PROPERTIES: A witch's herb used in flying ointment and love spells. The leaves symbolize love, money, health, power, and wisdom.

MEDICINAL PROPERTIES: Astringent and anti-inflammatory. Treats dysentery, sore throats, headaches, and menstrual cramps.

HOME: Make a floor wash with cinquefoil to wash away hexes and baneful energy.

RITUALS: Bathe with cinquefoil leaves for spiritual cleansing and prophetic dreams. Drink cinquefoil tea to revive body and spirit.

For the most potent herbal properties, gather cinquefoil when the moon is in Sagittarius.

CINNAMON

PLANET: SUN.   ELEMENT: FIRE.

MAGICAL PROPERTIES:
Spirituality, healing, and protection. One of the ancient world's most revered ceremonial and medicinal herbs.

MEDICINAL PROPERTIES: Stabilizes blood sugar and lowers blood pressure. Improves digestion and circulation. Warming, anti-microbial, and anti-fungal.

KITCHEN: Drink cinnamon tea or bake cinnamon bread to evoke the element of fire.

RITUALS: Use as an anointing oil in ceremony and burn as an incense to raise the energy and spiritual vibration in your sacred space.

"The toad will be much under sage, the frog will be in cinquefoil."

CLOVES

PLANET: JUPITER. ELEMENT: FIRE.

MAGICAL PROPERTIES: Protection, banishing, love, and money.

MEDICINAL PROPERTIES: A stimulant herb. Anti-parasitic and antiseptic. Used as a Southeast Asian medicinal staple for thousands of years.

KITCHEN: Use cloves in cooking and kitchen spells to protect your home and family, and draw in abundance.

SPELLCRAFT: Burn as an incense or anoint candles with clove oil to banish negative energy and purify your space. The scent of cloves will stop gossip or unwanted energy sent your way.

A charm bag full of cloves will attract love and abundance when carried in your pocket.

CLARY SAGE

PLANET: MERCURY. ELEMENT: AIR.

MAGICAL PROPERTIES: Clarity, vision, divination, and wisdom. Awakens the wisdom of the sages and the subtleties of the subconscious.

MEDICINAL PROPERTIES: Clary sage balances hormones, relieves PMS and some side effects of menopause. Do not ingest if pregnant.

SELF-CARE: Drink clary sage tea to uplift your spirit and reinvigorate your vision and purpose in life.

SPELLCRAFT: Anoint the third eye (and other chakras, if desired) with diluted clary sage oil. While reading tarot cards or engaging in meditative work, burn clary sage or diffuse the aromatic oil to induce a state of psychic sensitivity.

CYPRESS

PLANET: SATURN. ELEMENT: EARTH.

MAGICAL PROPERTIES: Immortality, life, death, and defense against sorcery. A powerful scent to lend strength in times of grief or crisis. Cypress is an ideal coffin wood for spiritual and practical purposes. A holy tree planted near temples and cemeteries in ancient times.

MEDICINAL PROPERTIES: The oil is astringent when applied externally.

GARDEN: Grow a cypress tree near your home for protection and magical energy.

HOME: Use protective cypress wood for your doors or store your magical supplies in a cypress wood chest.

RITUALS: Invoke the gods by burning dried cypress greenery. Wear a cypress crown to honor Pluto or hang a cypress sprig to ward off evil or negativity.

Alebrijes, a Oaxacan folkart, are often carved out of copal wood.

COPAL

PLANET: SUN. ELEMENT: FIRE.

Purchase copal incense from an ethical and sustainable source.

MAGICAL PROPERTIES: Known as the "incense tree" in Mayan and Aztec culture, copal is burned as an offering to the gods.

Sacred rites to celebrate the Aluxes, mythical spirits who guard the forest, are performed before harvesting copal.

MEDICINAL PROPERTIES: Copal treats skin disorders and irritations.

RITUALS: Burn copal resin to clear the air in your sacred space and remove energetic stagnation.

DAMIANA

PLANET: MARS.   **ELEMENT: FIRE.**

MAGICAL PROPERTIES: Love, lust, and magical power.

MEDICINAL PROPERTIES: Stimulant, aphrodisiac, and anti-depressant.

RITUALS: Burn damiana as incense or drink it as a tea to raise magical energy during spellwork or divination.

SELF-CARE: Drink a mood-lifting tea with lemon balm, damiana, and skullcap.

SPELLCRAFT: Store your quartz crystals with damiana and vice versa. They will protect and recharge each other's energy.

DITTANY
OF CRETE
PLANET: VENUS. ELEMENT: WATER.

Wild Dittany of Crete is rare, endangered, and protected from harvesting. Substitute with oregano or rose and bright green candles, or source this herb carefully from an ethical and sustainable source.

MAGICAL PROPERTIES: Calling in spirits and deities. Love and protection of the heart. A sacred plant in Hekate's garden.

SABBATS: Burn Dittany of Crete on Samhain to call spirits and lift the veil to the spirit world.

SELF-CARE: Drink the tea for a spiritual tonic.

SPELLCRAFT: Mix with vanilla, benzoin, and sandalwood to blend astral-projection incense. Burn with frankincense for spiritual protection or use in a sachet to attract love.

DANDELION

PLANET: JUPITER. ELEMENT: AIR.

MAGICAL PROPERTIES: Divination, calling spirits, and manifesting wishes.

MEDICINAL PROPERTIES: Detoxifying, prebiotic, and diuretic.

HOME: Brighten up your home or altar with yellow dandelion flowers.

KITCHEN: Eat a tonic salad of dandelion greens, marigold, and borage flowers to detoxify your digestive system.

RITUALS: Drink dandelion root tea to increase your divinatory powers.

SPELLCRAFT: Dry and roast the roots, then make tea for divination and psychic powers.

Blow a dandelion seed head and make a wish, or send a message to a spirit in this same way.

ELDER

PLANET: VENUS. ELEMENT: WATER.

MAGICAL PROPERTIES: Protection and counter-magic. Funeral rites, divination, and witch power. Sacred to the goddess Freya. An excellent wood for magic wands. The dead were often buried under elders in ancient times.

MEDICINAL PROPERTIES: Antiviral and anti-inflammatory. For thousands of years, people have used elder berries and flowers for herbal remedies to speed recovery from colds and flus. Also relieves the symptoms of allergies.

RITUALS: Elder trees are known to hold the spirits of faeries and witches. Kneel before the elder and honor it before cutting its wood.

GARDEN: Grow an elder near your home for protection and prosperity.

KITCHEN: Make elderflower vinegar, fritters, jams, and wine or tea. Steep elderflowers in lemon juice overnight, add water, and sweeten to taste for a sunny witch's brew.

SPELLCRAFT: Hang an elder wreath or charm at your door to counter any spells or hexes that come your way.

Place elder twigs under your pillow in the winter, and you'll have dreams to show what may come in spring when the elder blooms. Scatter elder leaves and flowers to the wind as you make a wish or send blessings to someone.

EUCALYPTUS
"GUM TREE"
PLANET: MOON. ELEMENT: WATER.

MAGICAL PROPERTIES: Healing powers, protection, and purification.

MEDICINAL PROPERTIES: An indigenous Australian herb. Traditional custodians used eucalyptus to treat coughs, colds, respiratory infections, and other illnesses. Today, eucalyptus is one of the most popular herbal medicinals and is used worldwide.

RITUALS: Burn eucalyptus leaves to clear the air for ritual or spellcasting.

SELF-CARE: Gently crush eucalyptus leaves, then boil them in water. Inhale the steam to relieve respiratory congestion. Drink eucalyptus tea for the same effect, or hang a sprig of eucalyptus in the shower. The leaves will release more of their oils when crushed or cracked.

SPELLCRAFT: Carry a small poppet or charm bag stuffed with eucalyptus leaves for protection and to maintain good health.

FENNEL

PLANET: MERCURY. ELEMENT: FIRE.

MAGICAL PROPERTIES: Protection, healing, purification, and power.

MEDICINAL PROPERTIES: Relieves digestive ailments and bloating.

KITCHEN: Crushed fennel seeds have been used to flavor food for millennia.

For a dash of all-purpose kitchen magic, mix Celtic sea salt with dried bay, basil, and fennel seeds. Add chili powder, if desired.

SABBATS: Use fennel in kitchen spells or in altar decorations for Litha and Lughnasadh. On Samhain, craft a protective crown or garland from nettle, rosemary, and fennel. Tie it with a black ribbon.

SPELLCRAFT: Hang fennel in windows and doors to protect your home from curses, especially those cast by malevolent elves. Wear a crown of fennel to increase your magical powers and protect your spirit. Or stuff a charm bag with fennel seeds to do the same.

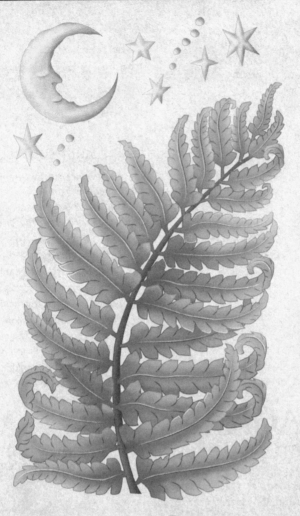

FERN

PLANET: MERCURY.   ELEMENT: AIR.

MAGICAL PROPERTIES: Invisibility, protection, luck, and magical visions.

HOME & GARDEN: Plant ferns around your house or at your doorstep to use their protective magic, or place ferns in bouquets indoors.

SABBATS: On the summer solstice, harvest fern seeds to attract wealth, or sit in a circle of ferns at midnight—Puck will appear and give you a purse of gold.

RITUALS: Find the first spring fern and you'll be blessed with luck for the upcoming season.

SPELLCRAFT: To enhance your chance of seeing faeries, rub wild thyme or fern seeds on your eyelids.

FRANKINCENSE

PLANET: SUN.   ELEMENT: FIRE.

Frankincense is threatened in the wild. Purchase from a sustainable source, or substitute with a combination of rose and rosemary or your favorite woody scent.

MAGICAL PROPERTIES: Divinity, protection, banishing, and spiritual connection.

Frankincense is an ancient ingredient in spiritual incense blends. It invokes spiritual power and focus for meditation and ritual.

RITUALS: Burn frankincense to subdue the ego and connect to the divine self.

SPELLCRAFT: Frankincense pairs well with topaz. Use frankincense to consecrate magic wands and other tools for summoning spiritual power.

FLY AGARIC

PLANET: MERCURY. ELEMENT: AIR.

POISON: Do not take internally or touch with your bare skin. This herb is best used symbolically, viewed in the wild, or substituted with red and white candles or nonpoisonous red flowers.

MAGICAL PROPERTIES: Flying, luck, visions, and magical power.

Opening portals to the spirit world and the world of the gnomes. A sacred mushroom in Siberian shamanic rituals.

SABBATS: Look for fly agaric under fir and spruce trees on the winter solstice. If you find them, you've also found a portal to the spirit world.

FRUIT BLOSSOM

PLANET: MOON. ELEMENT: WATER.

MAGICAL PROPERTIES: Love, partnership, and happiness. The powers of life and death.

KITCHEN: Make apple blossom tea, or use edible blossoms to garnish salads and sweets.

SPELLCRAFT: Make a sachet with orange or cherry blossoms to attract love. Bathe with orange, apple, or cherry blossoms to enhance your seductive qualities.

A blossom on the tree when the apples are ripe
Is a sure termination of somebody's life.
- An old legend of mortality.

GINGER

PLANET: MARS. ELEMENT: FIRE.

MAGICAL PROPERTIES:
Energy, abundance, and power. Some ancient people believed ginger came from the garden of Eden.

MEDICINAL PROPERTIES: Warming, antiseptic, and anti-inflammatory. One of the world's most powerful medicinal herbs, used in ancient Asian healing for thousands of years. Ginger helps to alleviate digestive issues, circulation, and respiratory issues.

KITCHEN: Make a special blend of green tea with ginger and ginseng. Brew yourself a cup whenever you need courage.

SELF-CARE: Drink ginger and lemon each day to revitalize and empower your body and spirit.

SPELLCRAFT: On a full moon, prepare a warming energy bath with fresh ginger, round orange slices, and a couple of drops of ylang-ylang oil. Submerge yourself underwater and ask for the energy to accomplish what you desire. When you emerge, you will be empowered and energized.

HAWTHORN

PLANET: MARS. ELEMENT: FIRE.

MAGICAL PROPERTIES:

Hawthorn symbolizes witch power and protection. Some witches can transform into hawthorn trees.

Hawthorn blossoms evoke feminine energy and a sense of the continuous renewal of nature. They are often found atop a maypole. Hawthorn is a sacred faerie tree.

GARDEN: Plant oak, ash, and hawthorn trees to create a portal to the faerie world. Hawthorn makes an excellent hedge for a witch's house.

RITUALS: Hold your rites under a hawthorn tree for extra magical power.

SABBATS: Use hawthorn or "May Flowers" in Beltane decorations, crowns, and spells.

SPELLCRAFT: Hang a hawthorn wreath on your door to keep out unwanted spirits.

HAZEL

PLANET: SUN. ELEMENT: AIR.

MAGICAL PROPERTIES: A sacred shrub associated with luck, protection, abundance, and wishes. Hazel is an excellent wood for making wands and divining rods. It protects from lightning and symbolizes the power of sacred fire.

SABBATS: Throw a hazelnut into the Samhain fire. If your nut crackles, you'll get what you desire.

SPELLCRAFT: Cast a magic circle with a hazelwood stick. String hazelnuts together and hang them to protect your house from unwanted spirits.

Wear a crown of hazelwood twigs and cast a spell for a wish to come true.

KITCHEN: Cook with hazelnuts for protection and abundance. Hazelnut pairs well with dark foods like chocolate, vanilla, and walnuts, as well as salt.

HENBANE

PLANET: SATURN. ELEMENT: WATER.

POISON: Do not take internally or touch with your bare skin. This herb is best used symbolically, viewed in the wild, or substituted with light yellow and dark red candles, nontoxic flowers, or ferns.

MAGICAL PROPERTIES:

Life, death, shape-shifting, spiritual visions, spellcasting power, and flight.

In Greek mythology, the dead were adorned with henbane before arriving in Hades, and the flowers were used to decorate graves.

Henbane was a common ingredient in traditional (and highly toxic) witch's flying ointment.

HEATHER

PLANET: VENUS. ELEMENT: WATER.

MAGICAL PROPERTIES: An ancient magical shrubbery. A symbol of love, luck, and protection, and also of loneliness, melancholy, and mourning.

An herb of immortality, life, and death. Perfect for cemeteries and soul-searching. The twigs of heather are a traditional material for witches' brooms.

BATH: On the full moon, draw a bath with heather petals and soak in it to increase your witch power.

GARDEN: Grow heather around your home for solitude and protection.

RITUALS: Burn dried heather to connect to the immortality of your soul, or place purple heather on your altar to call spirit guides. Make sachets of pink and white heather flowers to attract love.

SABBATS: Use heather to decorate for the first harvest (Lughnasadh) alongside grains and fruits.

HYSSOP

PLANET: JUPITER. ELEMENT: FIRE.

Hyssop essential oil can cause seizures in some. Work with the dried herb instead.

MAGICAL PROPERTIES: Protection and purification, especially for ritual.

HOME: Make a banishing floor wash with dried hyssop, lemon, vinegar, and salt.

RITUALS: Use a sprig of hyssop to sprinkle blessed water in ritual or to consecrate your magical tools.

SELF-CARE: Drink hyssop tea with honey to purify and enliven your spirit, or take a bath with dried hyssop, lavender, and salt.

SPELLCRAFT: For magical protection, hang sprigs of dried hyssop at your door.

Bundle a sprig of hyssop with an amethyst crystal to amplify both of their powers.

IVY

PLANET: SATURN.   ELEMENT: WATER.

Ivy is somewhat toxic. Do not ingest it.

MAGICAL PROPERTIES:

Protection, binding, strength, and luck. An ancient ritual herb used by the Druids, the feminine counterpart to the masculine holly.

HOME & GARDEN: Grow ivy to protect your home.

SPELLCRAFT: Carry a charm bag with ivy leaves for luck. Wear a crown of ivy for poetic inspiration or while making a wish. Cast your magic circle or bind a spell with ivy leaves and vines.

Ivy is a blessing for married couples, a symbol of binding their love. Victorian wedding rings were engraved with ivy.

Drops of lavender oil on your pillow will ease your mind and promote sleep.

"Lavande" means "to wash" in French.

LAVENDER

PLANET: MERCURY. ELEMENT: AIR.

MAGICAL PROPERTIES: Love, magic, purification, sleep, and peace.

MEDICINAL PROPERTIES: Anti-anxiety, antimicrobial, and antiseptic.

HOME: Scatter lavender flowers, burn the dried herb, or diffuse the oil to keep a sense of calm energy in your home.

KITCHEN: Bake a cake with lavender for someone you love.

SELF-CARE: Take a bath with lavender petals or drops of lavender oil to relieve stress. Drink lavender tea for the same effect. Smell fresh lavender often to retain a youthful spirit.

SPELLCRAFT: The scent or petals of lavender can be used in nearly any love spell. Crush lavender onto paper to enchant it with the energy of love. Write your desires on the paper, then burn it. Make a sachet of lavender and rosemary to stand calmly in your personal power.

LILAC

PLANET: VENUS. ELEMENT: WATER.

MAGICAL PROPERTIES: Protection and banishing of all evils and unwanted energy.

Lilac was known as "unlucky" by some because it was connected to witches and has an undeniably magical presence.

HOME & GARDEN: Grow lilac to protect your home from vengeful spirits.

Place lilacs indoors to drive out "ghosts" or lingering vibrations and moods.

SPELLCRAFT: Add a sprig of lilac to your witch's hat for spiritual protection.

To make a banishing water, mix a drop of lavender oil with spring water and leave it out under the full moon. Use a sprig of lilac to sprinkle this moon water in the "haunted" areas of your home.

LEMON BALM

"Melissa"

PLANET: MOON. ELEMENT: WATER.

MAGICAL PROPERTIES: Healing, love, comfort, and raising your spirits. Use it in a similar way to lavender — baths, teas, and sachets to attract love and provide a sense of calm and peace.

MEDICINAL PROPERTIES: Calming to the nervous system.

BATH: To release things on a dark moon, mix a sachet of sea salts, lemon balm, lavender, and kava-kava root. Prepare a bath, then submerge yourself in the water. When you emerge, you will leave behind what you wish to release.

HOME: Burn as incense or hang a sachet of the herb to cast healing energy.

SELF-CARE: Drink tea with lemon balm, skullcap, rose, and lavender to relieve cramps and stomach discomfort.

Craft a powerful wand with a stick from a lilac shrub.

MANDRAKE

PLANET: MERCURY. ELEMENT: FIRE.

TOXIC AND ENDANGERED: Do not take internally. This herb is often used symbolically or substituted with other dark roots like briony roots, and also apples, brown and green candles, tobacco, or ginger.

MAGICAL PROPERTIES: The most famous herb in magical history. Mandrake has legendary powers of spellcasting energy, manifestation, protection, exorcism, and love. A sacred herb of the ancient Egyptians. Mandrake is also a witch's herb and a favorite of the dark goddesses, Hekate and Circe.

HOME: Place a mandrake on your altar or mantle to protect your home and attract abundance.

SPELLCRAFT: Carve a mandrake or similar root with sigils, symbols, or words of power.

Soak mandrake root in spring water under the full moon. Sprinkle the water on your altar or magical workings to add power to any of your spells. Money placed with a mandrake root will double.

Mandrake can be tricky to grow. Are you willing to try? If so, keep it away from children and pets.

MISTLETOE

PLANET: SUN. ELEMENT: AIR.

POISON: Mistletoe berries are highly toxic. Do not ingest them, and keep them away from your children and pets.

MAGICAL PROPERTIES: Symbolizes luck, protection, and the triumph of life over death.

A sacred herb of the Druids, especially when found on an oak. A witch's herb that was also used in anti-witchcraft charms.

HOME: Hang a sprig of mistletoe to ward off misfortune and woe.

SABBATS: Harvest mistletoe with a golden sickle on the summer solstice or on the 6th day of the waning moon.

SPELLCRAFT: Hide a charm bag filled with mistletoe under your child's cradle to deter faeries from swapping them with a changeling. Make sure your child and pets cannot access the charm. Carry a bag of mistletoe for luck.

MINT

PLANET: MERCURY. ELEMENT: AIR.

MAGICAL PROPERTIES: Healing, protection, and abundance. An ancient magical herb.

MEDICINAL PROPERTIES: Antimicrobial and antibacterial. Soothes digestion, skin irritations, and headache.

HOME: Make a magical cleaning solution with spring water, mint tea, vinegar, and lemon.

SPELLCRAFT: Begin a manifestation on the dark moon by drinking tea with mint, burdock root, and star anise.

Crush a mint leaf and ask for divine assistance.

Take a bath or have some tea with mint, mugwort, and mullein to enhance your spellwork.

Stuff a poppet or cushion with mint leaves. Embroider symbols of what you wish to manifest on the outside.

MULLEIN

PLANET: SATURN. ELEMENT: FIRE.

MAGICAL PROPERTIES: Protection, courage, banishing, divination, and spellcasting power.

Witches made candles, torches, and "hag's tapers" out of mullein stalks and tips, and so mullein's power is illuminative to magical workings and rituals in general.

MEDICINAL PROPERTIES: An herb for coughs, respiratory, and bronchial issues.

RITUALS: Burn mullein to connect to the otherworldly realm. Ignite your ritual fire with dried mullein.

SABBATS: On Samhain, make mullein "hag's tapers" or burn the herb as incense to protect and illuminate your spirit work.

SPELLCRAFT: Mullein is an excellent substitute for graveyard dust.

MUGWORT

PLANET: VENUS. ELEMENT: EARTH.

MAGICAL PROPERTIES: Psychic and spiritual powers. An essential herb for divination tea, baths, and spirit work.

MEDICINAL PROPERTIES: Digestive and tonic. Do not ingest while pregnant.

RITUALS: Drink mugwort and mullein to enhance your connection to the other side. Burn mugwort and sandalwood to raise spiritual energy and protect your space.

Cast dried mugwort into a ritual fire and ask for visions and guidance.

SPELLCRAFT: Wear a crown of mugwort while performing spellwork or divination. Stuff a poppet with mugwort to charm it with spiritual energy. Wash your crystal ball with an infusion of mugwort to cleanse its energy. Scatter the herb beneath the ball to enhance your crystal's divinatory powers.

Dip dried mullein stalks in beeswax to make "hag's taper" candles.

MYRRH

PLANET: MOON. ELEMENT: WATER.

Myrrh is a rare tree in the wild and vulnerable to over-harvesting. Purchase from a sustainable source or substitute with vetivert and lavender.

MAGICAL PROPERTIES: Protection, spiritual energy, and banishing. Myrrh has been burned in temples and sacred spaces for thousands of years.

Myrrh is an excellent herb for maintaining presence in meditation and ritual. Myrrh is usually burned with frankincense as they compliment and enliven each other's magic.

MEDICINAL PROPERTIES: One of the oldest known medicines, myrrh was used for healing by the Egyptians and other ancient cultures. It is antiseptic, astringent, and anti-inflammatory.

RITUALS: Use myrrh's smoke to consecrate your tools or sacred space.

SELF-CARE: Myrrh represents the power of solitude and can be helpful in working through grief.

SPELLCRAFT: Make a tincture of myrrh and mint for a powerful mouthwash.

NETTLE

PLANET: MARS. ELEMENT: FIRE.

MAGICAL PROPERTIES: A plant of health and a witch's herb, famous for counter-magic, protection, and power.

MEDICINAL PROPERTIES: Tonic, astringent, anti-allergenic and anti-inflammatory.

BATH: Empower yourself in a bath of nettle leaves, salt, and peppermint oil.

KITCHEN: Combine nettle leaves, carrots, onions, garlic, and dandelion greens for a potent witch's soup.

RITUALS: Throw nettle into your ritual fire to cast a protective spell.

SELF-CARE: Tincture of root can soothe allergies and hives.

SPELLCRAFT: Use nettle for curse or hex removal. Burn it, carry it in a charm bag, or drink nettle tea.

HOME: Sprinkle dried nettle around your house to protect it energetically.

Sip nutmeg tea before tarot readings and divinations.

NUTMEG

PLANET: JUPITER. ELEMENT: FIRE.

Toxic in very large doses. Use sparingly.

MAGICAL PROPERTIES:

Luck, health, wealth, energetic power, and divination.

MEDICINAL PROPERTIES: Stimulant.

KITCHEN: Make a powerful pumpkin spice blend with nutmeg, cinnamon, cloves, and allspice. Bake gingerbread in shapes of what you desire, a manifestation spell used by witches for thousands of years.

RITUALS: Use nutmeg oil for anointing and consecrating tools and spell items.

SABBATS: Cook a Mabon pie with cinnamon, nutmeg, and cloves to enchant yourself with the spirit of autumn.

SPELLCRAFT: Anoint green or gold candles with olive oil and nutmeg. Burn the candles to manifest what you desire.

OAK

PLANET: SUN. ELEMENT: FIRE.

MAGICAL PROPERTIES: A sacred tree of the Druids and Romans. Oak is considered a tree of divinity and magic power. A tree with an undeniable spirit, the oak signifies strength, divinity, protection, life, and magic. The oak was a figure of cult worship in ancient times.

BATH: Make a "bath broom" or sachet with oak leaves, birch bark, and eucalyptus. Gently scrub your skin or place the broom in your hot bathwater.

SABBATS: Use oak leaves and acorns to decorate for Lughnasadh. Burn a cleansing ritual fire of oak wood on midsummer. Catch a falling oak leaf on Samhain and you won't catch a cold all winter.

SPELLCRAFT: Craft a powerful wand out of oak wood.

OLIVE

PLANET: SUN. ELEMENT: FIRE.

MAGICAL PROPERTIES: Life, strength, light, and divinity. Olive oil lit temples in ancient times. Olive is culinary, magical, and medicinal, and is the oldest farmed plant in the Mediterranean. Olive is a divine tree in a plethora of ancient cultures and is sacred to many gods and goddesses, notably, Athena.

MEDICINAL PROPERTIES: Olive leaf extract can help lower blood pressure and improve cardiovascular health. Olive oil is excellent for moisturizing dry skin.

BATH: Add 3-5 tablespoons of olive oil to your ritual bath or use it in your soap craft.

HOME: Hang a wreath of olive branches to protect your house and to bless your space on holy days.

SPELLCRAFT: Use olive oil to anoint tools, candles, and people. Carry olive leaves in a charm bag to increase luck and divine intervention.

PATCHOULI

PLANET: SATURN. ELEMENT: EARTH.

MAGICAL PROPERTIES: Wealth, prosperity, attracting love, and manifestation (bringing dreams to earth). A powerful, dark, earthy perfume oil for seduction and attraction.

MEDICINAL PROPERTIES: Aphrodisiac, antidepressant, and antiseptic.

HOME: Add dried patchouli to potpourri and bath sachets to enchant yourself with an aura of seduction.

RITUALS: Cast dried patchouli into a ritual fire and make a wish.

SABBATS: Blend a dark Samhain anointing oil with patchouli, cinnamon, and clove to use for manifestation power.

SPELLCRAFT: Anoint your handbag or wallet with oil of patchouli. Do the same with candles used in money spells.

PARSLEY

PLANET: MERCURY. ELEMENT: AIR.

MAGICAL PROPERTIES: Protection, purification, aphrodisiac, and dark magic. Parsley is associated with death and used in Greek funeral rites and veneration of graves. Sacred to Persephone.

MEDICINAL PROPERTIES: Parsley leaves are nutritious, tonic, and alleviate upset stomach.

BATH: A common ingredient in purification baths and baths to commune with spirit. Bathe with parsley, rue, and rosemary before a ritual.

KITCHEN: Use parsley alongside garlic and basil to enliven your spirit. Make tea with parsley, lemon balm, and nettle for the same effect.

SABBATS: An excellent herb for Samhain.

SPELLCRAFT: Make a crown of parsley to protect and enhance your spiritual connection.

PINE

PLANET: MARS. ELEMENT: AIR.

MAGICAL PROPERTIES:
Protection, cleansing, banishing, prosperity, and immortality (evergreen).

BATH: Take an invigorating bath with a handful of pine needles, Epsom salts, and three oranges cut into slices.

HOME: Burn pine needles or pine resin as a cleansing incense or as a counter-magic spell. For a magical cleansing potion, add sprigs of pine, juniper, and rosemary to your mop water.

SABBATS: Gather pine cones on the summer solstice and use them as decorations or garlands for Yule (winter solstice) as symbols of the sun.

"Sorcerer's Violet"

PERIWINKLE

PLANET: VENUS. ELEMENT: WATER.

MAGICAL PROPERTIES: Love, protection, witch's power, and the forces of life and death. A flower of sorcerers, poets, witches, and virgins. A traditional plant to make funeral wreaths in some customs.

HOME: Hang periwinkle over your door to protect and uplift the energy. Sprinkle periwinkle under your bed to attract love.

RITUALS: Cast periwinkles into a New Year's fire and make a wish.

SPELLCRAFT: Gather periwinkle only on the first, ninth, eleventh, or thirteenth night of the moon, and only after you've had a ritual bath to purify yourself.

Use periwinkles in remembrance of the dead and to recall lost memories.

*A stolen rose
will thrive.*

ROSE

PLANET: VENUS. ELEMENT: WATER.

MAGICAL PROPERTIES: Love, psychic power, beauty, and the powers of life and death.

"Rosary" beads come from the name "rose garden" in Latin and are symbolic of the many "petals" or prayers.

The rose is famous for the contrast between its beautiful blooms and sharp thorns.

MEDICINAL PROPERTIES: Oil of rose is mildly sedative and a gentle antidepressant.

BATH: Revitalize your spirit by adding rose petals to your bath or washing your face and hair with rosewater.

GARDEN: Plant miniature roses to attract faeries.

KITCHEN: Drink rosehip or rosebud tea before bed to have prophetic dreams.

RITUALS: Attract a lover by frolicking through the garden nude as you scatter rose petals. Cast a beautiful magic circle with rose petals.

SPELLCRAFT: Place a single rose on your altar to cast a love spell. String dried rosehips and hang them as a charm to attract love.

ROSEMARY

PLANET: SUN. ELEMENT: FIRE.

MAGICAL PROPERTIES: An all-purpose ritual herb known for adding protection, strength, and power to nearly any spell or occasion. A symbol of life and death.

MEDICINAL PROPERTIES: Astringent, tonic, stimulant, anti-inflammatory, and antioxidant.

BATH: Take a purifying magical bath with rosemary and parsley.

KITCHEN: A common culinary herb, have rosemary on hand to add power and energy to any of your kitchen spells.

SELF-CARE: Place rosemary under your pillow for restful sleep without nightmares.

SPELLCRAFT: Burning the dried herb evokes a powerful smoke for energetic clearing and receiving answers or divine guidance. Carry a sachet of rosemary anytime you need to amplify your personal power and luck. The scent of rosemary will help to increase your powers of focus and concentration. Place rosemary under your pillow to remember your dreams.

RUE

PLANET: MARS. ELEMENT: FIRE.

Toxic in excess. Never take while pregnant, and wear gloves while handling fresh rue.

MAGICAL PROPERTIES: Counter-magic and protective powers. Store rue with a ruby as they will charge and protect each other. An excellent herb for spiritual protection while practicing divination and spirit work.

HOME: Hang a small bunch in the kitchen to protect your space, or strew the dried herb mixed with salt in doorways and corners.

RITUALS: Use a sprig of rue to sprinkle saltwater as you cast a magic circle.

ROWAN

PLANET: SUN. ELEMENT: FIRE.

MAGICAL PROPERTIES: Protection, counter-magic, psychic powers, and spiritual visions. A witch's tree as well as a tree used to protect against witches. It can call spirits and also banish them, and so makes an excellent wand wood.

HOME: Rowan berries are a powerful addition to magical incense.

Cross two rowan sticks of equal length to make an ancient protective charm.

RITUALS: Ask the goddess for help and wisdom by praying under a rowan tree.

SABBATS: One of the nine sacred woods of the Beltane fire (birch, rowan, ash, alder, willow, hawthorn, oak, holly, and hazel).

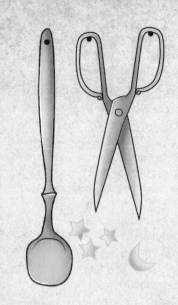

SANDALWOOD

PLANET: MOON. ELEMENT: WATER.

Sandalwood is a vulnerable and protected species. Source from ethical and sustainable sources, or use vetivert or another sweet, woody scent instead.

MAGICAL PROPERTIES: Full moon power, spiritual vibration, protection, and counter-magic. Calms the mind and increases confidence.

MEDICINAL PROPERTIES: Antiseptic. Soothes skin. Sandalwood is used extensively in both traditional Chinese and Ayurvedic medicine.

RITUALS: Raises the vibration in any type of ritual, meditation, or spirit work. Throw a chip of sandalwood into a ritual fire and make a wish.

SABBATS: Conjure spirits on Samhain with a mix of lavender and sandalwood.

SPELLCRAFT: Wear sandalwood beads or charms for a protective magical amulet.

SAGE

PLANET: JUPITER. ELEMENT: AIR.

MAGICAL PROPERTIES: Wisdom, healing, protection, and purification.

MEDICINAL PROPERTIES: An essential medicinal herb in the ancient Mediterranean. Sage's official name, salvia, is derived from a word meaning "to heal" in Latin. Antiseptic, astringent, nerve tonic. An excellent remedy for sore throat and stomach.

GARDEN: Grow sage, nasturtium, thyme, and hyssop to protect your garden from insects.

KITCHEN: Use sage for warmth and wisdom in recipes and kitchen witchcraft.

Sage pairs well with eggplant, garlic, mushrooms, stuffing, and cheese. Use parsley, sage, rosemary, thyme, and salt as an all-purpose kitchen spell.

SPELLCRAFT: Carry sage leaves to glean wisdom and manifest money. Sage twigs and leaves are excellent for bundling into a small magical broom.

To make a dream come true, write your wish on a sage leaf and place it under your pillow. Sleep on the leaf for three nights, then bury it.

Sandalwood improves your Qi (Chi) energy flow.

SKULLCAP

PLANET: SATURN. ELEMENT: WATER.

MAGICAL PROPERTIES: Peace and relaxation. Commitment and fidelity. An excellent herb for handfasting ceremonies and binding yourself to something for the long term.

MEDICINAL PROPERTIES: Sedative, nerve tonic, and a mild bitter. A powerful herb for menstrual health in Native American medicine.

BATH: Add skullcap, lavender, and Epsom salts to your bath to relieve stress and bring on a state of peace.

SELF-CARE: Take a tincture or tea of skullcap to de-stress your nervous system and promote peaceful sleep.

ST. JOHN'S WORT

PLANET: SUN. ELEMENT: FIRE.

MAGICAL PROPERTIES: The power of the sun. Protection against sadness.

MEDICINAL PROPERTIES: Anti-viral, anti-depressant, anti-inflammatory, and nerve tonic.

RITUALS: Burn the flowers to evoke fire spirits and communicate with the element of fire. Drink St. John's Wort tea to lift your spirits.

SABBATS: Gather at noon on the summer solstice for the most magical power and sunny strength. Cast into your summer solstice fire for protection.

SLIPPERY ELM

PLANET: SATURN. ELEMENT: AIR.

MAGICAL PROPERTIES: Counter-magic. Stops gossip, ill will, and negative energy from harming you.

MEDICINAL PROPERTIES: The infusion of bark is excellent for coughs and upset stomach. A powerful healing herb in native North American traditions.

SELF-CARE: Mix a healing tea for coughs and colds with slippery elm bark, licorice root, marshmallow root, orange peel, and lemon.

SPELLCRAFT: Burn slippery elm to deflect any negative energy sent your way.

SUNFLOWER

PLANET: SUN. ELEMENT: FIRE.

MAGICAL PROPERTIES: The power of solar energy and immortality of spirit. Happiness and prosperity. The ancient Aztecs and Incas used sunflowers as a ritual herb to honor the sun god.

BATH: Add sunflower petals, chamomile flowers, and Epsom salt to your bath to instill a sense of happiness and renewed spirit.

GARDEN: Grow sunflowers for a (relatively!) easy and impressive bit of garden magic.

KITCHEN: Use the delicious seeds for snacks and salads, or add a few petals to your dish for depth of flavor and a sunny-colored accent.

SABBATS: Place sunflowers on your altar to represent solar deities on the solstices.

STAR ANISE

PLANET: JUPITER. ELEMENT: AIR.

Chinese star anise is a common culinary spice. Japanese star anise, while sacred, is toxic.

MAGICAL PROPERTIES: Luck, spiritual energy, and psychic powers.

KITCHEN: Toss a magical, spicy star into soup, tea, or chocolaty desserts.

SABBATS: Stitch or glue the pods onto a ribbon to craft starry solstice garlands. Make dark divination tea on Samhain with star anise, black tea, cinnamon, and a hint of chocolate and cream. For love divination, add licorice root.

SPELLCRAFT: Burn star anise seeds as incense to set a spiritual vibe. Carry an anise star as a good luck charm.

THYME

PLANET: VENUS. ELEMENT: WATER.

MAGICAL PROPERTIES: Protection, courage, psychic powers, and health.

A potent ritual and purification herb used in ancient Greek temples.

Thyme is culinary, magical, and medicinal.

MEDICINAL PROPERTIES: Tonic, anti-oxidant, and antiseptic. Thyme tea can also soothe and prevent the common cold.

RITUALS: Burn thyme to assist in contacting spirits. Bathe in thyme and marjoram to clear lingering energy of the past. Drink thyme tea to increase your vitality.

SPELLCRAFT: Burn or consume thyme for protection. Wear a sprig of thyme on your witch's hat for courage and glamour.

TANSY

PLANET: VENUS. ELEMENT: WATER.

Toxic. Do not ingest.

MAGICAL PROPERTIES: Immortality of the soul. Connection to the divine feminine and sacred mother.

SPELLCRAFT: Place a bouquet of tansy on your altar to represent your goddess or the divine feminine. A classic flower to pick and give to your mother.

As written in an herbal from the 1500s, women would gather tansy, wormwood, and mugwort on St. John the Baptist's day (August 15th) "and use it for practicing very strange idolatries and all sorts of madness." Perform this ritual next August.

VANILLA

PLANET: VENUS. ELEMENT: WATER.

MAGICAL PROPERTIES: Love, lust, and the divine feminine. Vanilla restores your personal vitality and increases your powers of attraction.

BATH: Add milk, vanilla, and orange slices to your bath to make yourself irresistibly sweet and attractive.

KITCHEN: Use vanilla to attract passionate romance. Make vanilla-scented sugar by placing a vanilla bean in a witchy sugar jar.

SPELLCRAFT: Vanilla beans are popular ingredients in poppets and charm bags to attract love. Use vanilla in spells to soothe emotional pain caused by fighting.

VALERIAN

PLANET: VENUS. ELEMENT: WATER.

MAGICAL PROPERTIES: Love, sleep, protection, and purification. A witch's healing herb.

MEDICINAL PROPERTIES: Calming, sedative, relaxant, and anti-anxiety. Provides relief for menstrual symptoms. Valerian was known as "all-heal" and "wonder root" in ancient times, as it cured so many conditions.

BATH: Mix valerian root, skullcap, and lavender for a powerful peace-inducing bath.

SELF-CARE: Drink valerian root tea to calm your nerves, soothe anxiety, and relax the anxious mind.

SPELLCRAFT: Valerian is powerful in spells to attract love. Make a ceremonial broom to clear the energy of your space with a hazelwood handle and a brush made of vervain, periwinkle, sage, mint, valerian, ash, and basil.

Burn your tongue? A drop of vanilla can ease the pain.

VETIVERT

PLANET: VENUS. ELEMENT: EARTH.

MAGICAL PROPERTIES: Uplifting, healing, and protective. A sacred herb in ancient Hindu ritual.

"I am the fragrance of the soil." -Krishna, from the Bhagavad Gita.

MEDICINAL PROPERTIES: A traditional herb in Ayurvedic medicine. Known as "oil of tranquility," vetivert promotes restful sleep and calms anxiety.

SELF-CARE: Make a soothing tea with vetivert root, chocolate, and mint.

SPELLCRAFT: Burn vetivert root to protect and relax the energy of your space. Make a charm bag with vetivert roots, a few drops of vanilla, and a small rose quartz heart to attract love.

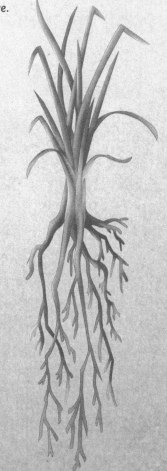

VERBENA

PLANET: VENUS. ELEMENT: EARTH.

MAGICAL PROPERTIES: Love, protection, divination, and purification. A symbol of devotion and the sweetness of magic. Verbena was a sacred herb of the ancient Druids, Greeks, and Romans, and is associated with the worship of many gods and goddesses.

MEDICINAL PROPERTIES: A mild bitter, tonic, and anti-depressant.

RITUALS: Make a small bundle of verbena and use it as an altar-clearing ritual broom.

SABBATS: Gather verbena on the summer solstice for the strongest magical qualities. Cast verbena, mugwort, and vervain into your solstice fire while you make a wish.

SELF-CARE: Drink verbena tea or add it to your bath to relieve stress.

SPELLCRAFT: Wear a crown of verbena to amplify your magical energy.

Mix black lava salt, rose petals, and vetivert in a bath to ground your spirit.

WITCH HAZEL

PLANET: SUN. ELEMENT: FIRE.

MAGICAL PROPERTIES: Protection, magic, and divination. A wood used in ancient divining rods.

MEDICINAL PROPERTIES:
A traditional healing herb in Native American medicine. Astringent and anti-inflammatory. Tinctures and ointments made of witch hazel bark are excellent for treating skin.

SELF-CARE: Use witch hazel in homemade soaps, facial cleansers, and shower scrubs. Pairs well magically and medicinally with tea tree oil.

SPELLCRAFT: Make a spellcasting wand out of a witch hazel twig. Mix witch hazel with drops of mugwort and clary sage oil to use as a divination or spiritual spritz.

WORMWOOD

PLANET: MARS. ELEMENT: FIRE.

Toxic in excess amounts. Use sparingly.

MAGICAL PROPERTIES: Psychic powers, communication with spirits, and spiritual protection. An ancient and sacred ritual herb, handed down from the gods.

MEDICINAL PROPERTIES: An aromatic bitter. Anti-inflammatory, antimicrobial, and mildly antidepressant.

RITUALS: Burn as incense for spirit-work and to raise your own spirits. Often mixed with sandalwood for use in séance.

SABBATS: Drink a spiritually-elevating tea on Samhain, such as wormwood or a blend of mugwort, yarrow, and lavender.

SPELLCRAFT: Carry wormwood to protect yourself from sea serpents and all that is evil.

WOODRUFF

PLANET: MARS. ELEMENT: FIRE.

MAGICAL PROPERTIES: Protection, success, and abundance. Woodruff's delicate white flowers represent the beginning of spring. Associated with the goddess Freya.

MEDICINAL PROPERTIES: Tonic and anti-inflammatory. Toxic for some in high doses.

BATH: Add a bit of dried woodruff to a ceremonial "milk and honey" bath in early spring to cleanse and enliven your spirit.

KITCHEN: Make "May wine"—a traditional Germanic drink to celebrate Beltane, or make a soothing cup of woodruff tea with honey.

SPELLCRAFT: Woodruff attracts money when carried in your handbag. Bundle woodruff flowers and St. John's wort as a protective bouquet. A sweet, hay-like scent makes woodruff an excellent sachet herb alongside lavender to scent your clothes and closet.

Wormwood makes a lovely insect repellent.

YARROW

PLANET: VENUS. ELEMENT: WATER.

MAGICAL PROPERTIES: Counter-magic, love, and spiritual powers.

MEDICINAL PROPERTIES: A classic European herb of healing. Astringent, tonic, anti-inflammatory. Useful for treating allergies and the common cold.

BATH: Add yarrow tea to your bath to cleanse and enliven your spirit.

HOME: Hang a bundle of yarrow to uplift and protect your spirit and send back hexes. Or mix dried yarrow with salt and sprinkle in doorways.

RITUALS: Drink yarrow tea to increase your spiritual connection.

SABBATS: Use yarrow in summer solstice garlands and decorations.

YEW

PLANET: SATURN. ELEMENT: WATER.

Extremely toxic. Do not consume or leave in reach of pets or children.

MAGICAL PROPERTIES: Sacred to the Druids. Often planted on holy sites and graveyards. A symbol of life, death, and immortality. Yew makes an excellent wand wood, however, due to its toxicity, it must be handled, crafted, and stored with care. A tree commonly associated with Hekate and other dark goddesses.

RITUALS: Visit an ancient yew tree. Collect berries or needles as they fall from the tree, before they hit the ground. Seal them in an airtight bottle. Open the bottle once to unleash a powerful force of life into your spellwork.

HERBS & THE ELEMENTS

EARTH

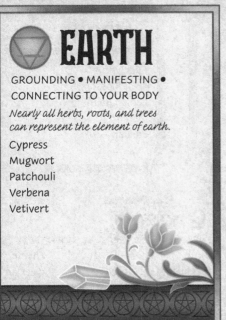

GROUNDING • MANIFESTING •
CONNECTING TO YOUR BODY

*Nearly all herbs, roots, and trees
can represent the element of earth.*

Cypress
Mugwort
Patchouli
Verbena
Vetivert

AIR

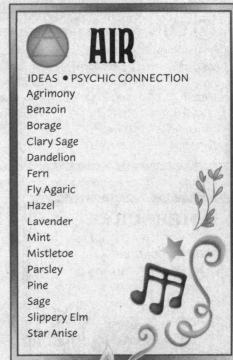

IDEAS • PSYCHIC CONNECTION

Agrimony
Benzoin
Borage
Clary Sage
Dandelion
Fern
Fly Agaric
Hazel
Lavender
Mint
Mistletoe
Parsley
Pine
Sage
Slippery Elm
Star Anise

WATER

EMOTIONS • INTUITION

Aconite	Sandalwood
Belladonna	Skullcap
Birch	Tansy
Blackberry	Thyme
Burdock	Valerian
Chamomile	Vanilla
Dittany of Crete	Yarrow
Elder	Yew
Eucalyptus	
Fruit Blossom	
Heather	
Henbane	
Ivy	
Lemon Balm	
Lilac	
Myrrh	
Periwinkle	
Rose	

FIRE

PASSION • PURPOSE • ACTION

Amaranth	Hyssop
Angelica	Mandrake
Basil	Mullein
Bay	Nettle
Betony	Nutmeg
Blackthorn	Oak
Calendula	Olive
Cinnamon	Rosemary
Cinquefoil	Rowan
Cloves	Rue
Copal	St. John's Wort
Damiana	Sunflower
Fennel	Witch Hazel
Frankincense	Sweet Woodruff
Ginger	Wormwood
Hawthorn	

HERBS & THE PLANETS

☉ SUN ENERGY OF THE SELF & THE DIVINE

Amaranth	Copal	Rowan
Angelica	Frankincense	St. John's Wort
Bay	Hazel	Sunflower
Benzoin	Mistletoe	Sweet Woodruff
Calendula	Oak	Witch Hazel
Chamomile	Olive	
Cinnamon	Rosemary	

*The sun and moon are called "planets" in astrology.

☽ MOON

ENERGY OF THE SUBCONSCIOUS

Eucalyptus
Fruit Blossom
Lemon Balm
Myrrh
Sandalwood

☿ MERCURY

ENERGY OF THE MIND, IDEAS,
& COMMUNICATIONS

Clary Sage	Mandrake
Fennel	Mint
Fern	Parsley
Fly Agaric	
Lavender	

♀ VENUS

ENERGY OF LOVE, PLEASURE, & CREATIVITY

Birch	Heather	Thyme
Blackberry	Lilac	Valerian
Burdock	Mugwort	Vanilla
Dittany of	Periwinkle	Verbena
Crete	Rose	Vetivert
Elder	Tansy	Yarrow

♂ MARS

ENERGY OF ACTION

Basil	Nettle
Blackthorn	Pine
Damiana	Rue
Ginger	Wormwood
Hawthorn	

♃ JUPITER

ENERGY OF EXPANSION

Agrimony	Hyssop
Betony	Nutmeg
Borage	Sage
Cinquefoil	Star Anise
Cloves	
Dandelion	

♄ SATURN

ENERGY OF FOCUS, STRUCTURE, & CONTRACTION

Aconite	Patchouli
Belladonna	Skullcap
Cypress	Slippery
Henbane	Elm
Ivy	Yew
Mullein	

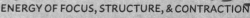

HERBS & THE SABBATS

SAMHAIN — Oct. 31

Agrimony
Blackthorn
Dittany of Crete
Fennel
Hazel
Mullein
Mugwort

Oak
Parsley
Patchouli
Sandalwood
Star Anise
Wormwood

YULE — Dec. 21
Winter Solstice

Bay
Blackthorn
Fly Agaric
Frankincense
Ivy
Mistletoe
Myrrh

Oak
Pine
Star Anise

* If you live in the Southern Hemisphere (Australia, etc.), all dates will shift by six months (June instead of December, and so on.)

IMBOLC — Feb. 1

Angelica
Basil
Bay
Birch
Bramble (Blackberry)
Cedar
Rowan

OSTARA — Mar. 21
Spring Equinox

Birch
Fruit Blossom
Lilac
Periwinkle
Rose
Yew

BELTANE — May 1

Blackthorn
Elder
Hawthorn
Hazel
Oak
Rowan
Sweet Woodruff

LITHA (MIDSUMMER) — June 21
Summer Solstice

Basil
Calendula
Chamomile
Elder
Fennel
Fern
Mistletoe

Pine
Mugwort
Oak
St. John's Wort
Verbena
Vervain
Yarrow

LUGHNASADH — Aug. 1

Basil
Blackberry
Fennel
Heather
Oak
Rowan
Yarrow

MABON — Sept 21
Autumnal Equinox

Blackthorn
Cinnamon
Cloves
Fern
Hazel
Sage
Nutmeg

HERBAL INTENTIONS

COUNTER-MAGIC & HEX-BREAKING

Aconite
Agrimony
Angelica
Chamomile
Cloves
Cypress
Elder

Frankincense
Mullein
Myrrh
Nettle
Pine
Rowan
Rue

Sandalwood
Slippery Elm
Yarrow

HEALTH & HEALING

Agrimony
Amaranth
Blackberry
Burdock
Cinnamon
Eucalyptus
Fennel

Lemon Balm
Mint
Nutmeg
Rosemary
St. John's Wort
Thyme
Vetivert

IMMORTALITY, LIFE, AND DEATH

Amaranth
Belladonna
Blackthorn
Cypress
Elder
Fruit Blossom
Heather

Henbane
Mistletoe
Oak
Olive
Periwinkle
Pine
Rose

Rosemary
Sunflower
Tansy
Yew

LOVE

Cinquefoil
Cloves
Damiana
Dittany of Crete
Fruit Blossom
Heather
Lavender

Lemon Balm
Mandrake
Parsley
Patchouli
Periwinkle
Rose
Skullcap

Valerian
Vanilla
Verbena
Yarrow

LUCK

Benzoin
Fern
Ginger
Hazel
Heather
Ivy
Mistletoe

Nutmeg
Olive
Star Anise

MANIFESTATION & WEALTH

Basil
Blackthorn
Cinquefoil
Cloves
Dandelion
Ginger
Hazel

Mandrake
Mint
Nutmeg
Patchouli
Pine
Sunflower
Vanilla

Sweet Woodruff

HERBAL INTENTIONS

PEACE

Benzoin
Borage
Calendula
Chamomile

Lavender
Lemon Balm
Sandalwood
Skullcap

St. John's
Wort
Valerian
Vetivert

PROTECTION

Many herbs can be used for protection.
Write your favorites here.

PSYCHIC POWERS & VISIONS

Aconite
Bay
Belladonna
Borage
Calendula
Clary Sage
Copal
Dandelion
Dittany of Crete

Elder
Fern
Fly Agaric
Henbane
Mandrake
Mugwort
Mullein
Myrrh
Nutmeg

Parsley
Rose
Rowan
Rue
Sage
Sandalwood
St. John's
Wort
Star Anise

Thyme
Verbena
Witch Hazel
Wormwood
Yarrow

PURIFICATION & ENERGY CLEARING

Angelica
Basil
Bay
Betony
Birch
Blackberry
Calendula
Clary Sage
Copal
Eucalyptus
Fennel
Frankincense
Hyssop
Lavender
Lilac
Mint
Myrrh
Olive
Parsley

Pine
Rue
Sage
Sandalwood
Thyme
Valerian
Verbena
Witch Hazel

SPIRITUALITY & DIVINITY

Aconite
Amaranth
Benzoin
Calendula
Cinnamon
Clary Sage
Copal
Cypress

Dittany of Crete
Fly Agaric
Frankincense
Heather
Myrrh
Oak
Olive
Parsley

Star Anise
Sunflower
Verbena
Yarrow
Yew

WITCH POWER

Aconite
Basil
Belladonna
Benzoin
Blackthorn
Borage
Cinquefoil
Cypress
Damiana

Elder
Fennel
Fly Agaric
Ginger
Hawthorn
Henbane
Lavender
Mandrake
Mistletoe

Mugwort
Mullein
Nettle
Oak
Parsley
Periwinkle
Rosemary
Rowan
Tansy

Valerian
Verbena
Witch Hazel
Wormwood
Yew

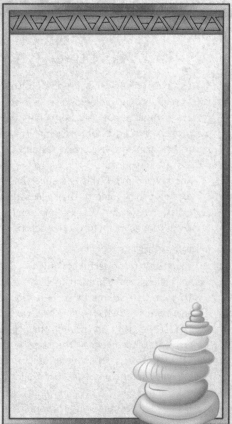

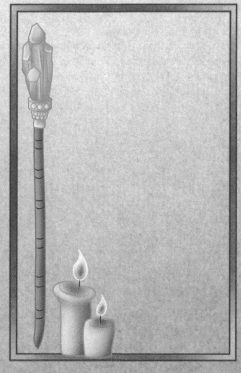

Spellcasting Basics

There are opening and closing steps that are basic accompaniments to spells in this book. These steps are optional but advisable: at least know "why" many witches perform these processes and try them out for yourself.

And keep in mind, this is a super basic "coloring book" guide to the spellcasting process. There are books and online sources that go much further in-depth.

THE SECRET OF SPELLS

The secret to powerful spells is in you. Your feeling and vibration in alignment with your true source of self—and/or a higher power—is what makes spells work.

The secret isn't in having the right ingredients and doing all the steps in a particular order. It's in your ability to focus your intent and use your feelings, mind, and soul to call in what you want—to harness the energy of yourself in harmony with the Earth, stars, moon, planets, or whatever other spiritual forces you call upon.

BREAK THE RULES

The first rule is to throw out any of the rules that don't work for you. Do things that feel right, significant, and meaningful. Adapt spells from different practices, books, and teachers. The only way to know what works is to follow your curiosity and try things out.

USING TOOLS

Your feelings and vibration are what unlocks the magic, not the tools, exact words, or sequences. You can cast amazing spells for free with no tools at all, and you can cast an elaborate spell that yields no results.

That said, tools like herbs, oils, crystals, and cauldrons can be powerful and fun to use in your spells. Just don't feel pressured or discouraged if you don't have much to start. Keep your magic straightforward and powerful. The right tools and ingredients will come.

"AS ABOVE, SO BELOW"

Tools, ingredients, and symbols are based on the magical theory of sympathetic magic and correspondence. You might hear the phrase, "As Above, So Below," which means the spiritual qualities of objects are passed down to earth. It's "sympathetic magic," or "this equals that," like how a figure of a lion represents that power but is not an actual lion.

Start by following lists, charts, and spells to get a feel for what others use and then begin to discover your own meaningful symbolism and correspondences.

PERMISSION

Spellbooks are like guidelines. They should be modified, simplified, or embellished to your liking. And don't degrade your magic by calling it "lazy." Keeping your witchcraft simple is okay. Go ahead, you have permission.

Also, it's not a competition to see who can use the most esoteric stuff in their spell. Hooray! It's about finding your personal power and style.

SPELLCASTING OUTLINE:

1. Plan and prepare.
2. Cast a circle.
3. Ground and center.
4. Invoke a deity or connection to self.
5. Raise energy.
6. Do your spellcraft (like the spells in this book).
7. Ground and center again.
8. Close your circle.
9. Clean up.
10. Act in accord (and be patient!).

1. PLAN AND PREPARE: If you're doing a written spell, read it several times to get familiar with it. Decide if there's anything you'll substitute or change. If you're writing your own spell, enjoy the process and mystery of seeing the messages and theme come together.

Gather all of the items you'll be using (if any) and plan out space and time where you'll do the spell. Spells can be impromptu, so preparations can be quick and casual if you like.

2. CAST A CIRCLE AND CALL THE QUARTERS: A magic circle is a container to collect the energy of your spell. Circles are also protective, as they form a ring or "barrier" around you. Circles can elevate your space to a higher vibration and clear out unwanted energy before you begin. Calling the Quarters is done to get the universal energy of the elements flowing. Incense is typically burned at the same time to purify the air and energy. If you

can't burn things, that's ok. If you've never cast a circle, try it. It's a mystical experience like no other. Once you have a few candles lit and start to walk around it, magic does happen!

HOW TO CAST A CIRCLE: This is a basic, bare-bones way to cast a circle. It's often much more elaborate, and this explanation barely does it justice, so read up to find out more. And note that while some cast the circle first and then call the Quarters, some do it the other way around.

1. Hold out your hand, wand, or crystal, and imagine a white light and a sphere of pure energy surrounding your space, as you circle around clockwise three times. Your circle can be large or it can be tiny, just space for you and your materials.

2. Call the Four Quarters or Five Points of the Pentagram, depending on your preferences. The Quarters (also known as the Elements!) are Earth (North), Air (East), Fire (South), and Water (West). Many use the Pentagram and also call the 5th Element, Spirit or Self.

Face in each direction and say a few words to welcome the element. For example, "To the North, I call upon your power of grounding and strength. To the East, I call upon the source of knowledge. To the South, I call upon your passion and burning desire to take action. To the West, I call upon the intuition of emotion. To the Spirit and Source of Self, I call upon your guidance and light."

3. GROUND AND CENTER: Grounding and centering prepare you to use the energy from the Earth, elements, and universe. Most witches agree that if you skip these steps, you'll be drawing off of your own energy, which can be exhausting and ineffective. It's wise to ground and center both before and after a spell. It's like the difference between being "plugged into" the magical energy of the Earth and universe versus "draining your batteries."

HOW TO GROUND AND CENTER:

To ground, imagine the energy coming up from the core of the Earth and into your feet, as you breathe deeply. You can visualize deep roots from your feet all the way into the center of the Earth, with these roots drawing the Earth's energy in and out of you. The point is to allow these great channels of energy to flow through you and into your spell. You can also imagine any of your negative energy, thoughts, or stress leaving.

To center, once you've got a good flow of energy from the ground, imagine the energy shining through and out the top of your head as a pure form of your highest creative self and then back in as the light of guidance. Suspend yourself here between the Earth and the sky, supported with the energy flowing freely through you, upheld, balanced, cleansed, and "in flow" with the energy of the universe. This process takes just a couple of minutes.

4. INVOKE A DEITY OR CREATIVE SOURCE: If you'd like to invoke a deity or your highest self to help raise energy and your vibration, call upon them. Invoking deities is way deeper than this book, so research it more if it calls to you!

5. RAISE ENERGY: The point of raising energy is to channel the universal (magical!) forces you tapped into through the previous steps to use in your spell. And raising energy is fun. You can sing, dance, chant, meditate, or do breath work. You want to do something that feels natural, so you can really get into it, lose yourself, and raise your state of consciousness.

A good way to start is to chant "Ong," allowing the roof of your mouth to vibrate ever so slightly. This vibration changes up the energy in your mind, body, and breath and is a simple yet powerful technique.

Another tip is to raise energy to the point of the "peak" where you feel it at its highest. Don't go too far where you start to tucker out or lose enthusiasm!

6. DO YOUR SPELL: Your spell can be as simple as saying an intention and focusing on achieving the outcome of what you want, or it can be more elaborate. Whichever way you prefer, do what feels right to you.

TIPS ON VISUALIZATION AND INTENTION:

Most spellwork involves a bit of imagination and intention, and here are some subtleties you can explore.

The Power of You The most important tool in magic is you. You've got it—both power right now and vast untapped power that you can explore. To cast a successful spell, you've got to focus your mind and genuinely feel the emotions and feelings of the things you want to manifest.

If you haven't started meditating in some form yet, start now! It's not too late, and it's easier than you think.

Visualize the Outcome

Visualization doesn't have to be visual. In fact, *feeling* the outcome of what you want may be more effective than seeing it (try both). And try to feel or see the *completion* of your desire without worrying about the process or *how* you'll get there.

If you don't know how you're going to achieve your goal (yet!) it can feel overwhelming when you try to visualize how you're going to pull it off. Instead, feel the sense of calm, completion, and control that you'll feel *after* you achieve it.

Phrase it Positively

Another tip is to phrase your intentions and desires positively. You're putting energy into this, so make sure the intention is going to be good for you. Instead of saying what you don't want, "to get out of my bad job that I hate," phrase it positively, "I want to do something that's fulfilling with my career."

Then you'll be able to feel good about it as you visualize and cast your spell.

7. GROUND AND CENTER AGAIN

After your spell, it's important to ground out any excess energy. Do this again by visualizing energy flowing through you and out. You can also imagine any "extra" energy you have petering out as you release it back into the Earth.

8. CLOSE YOUR CIRCLE

If you called the Quarters or a deity, let them know the spell has ended by calling them out again, with thanks if desired.

Close your circle the opposite of how you opened it, circling around three times or more counterclockwise. Then say, "This circle is closed," or do a closing chant or song to finish your spell.

9. CLEAN UP

Don't be messy with your magic! Put away all of your spell items.

10. ACT IN ACCORD: Once you have cast your spell, you've got to take action. You can cast a spell to become a marine biologist, but if you don't study for it, it's never going to happen. So take action towards what you want to open the possibility for it to come.

Look for signs, intuition, and coincidences that point you in the direction of your desires. If you get inspired after a spell, take action! Don't be surprised if you ask for money and then come up with a new idea to make money. Follow those clues, especially if they feel exciting and good.

If your spell comes true, discard and "release" any charm bag, poppet, or item you used to hold and amplify energy. Also, give thanks (if that's in your practice) or repay the universe in some way, doing something kind or of service that you feel is a solid trade for what you received from your spell.

WHAT IF YOUR SPELL DOESN'T WORK?

It's true that not all spells will work! But sometimes the results just take longer than you'd like, so be patient.

If your spell doesn't work, you can use divination or meditation to do some digging into reasons why.

The good news is your own magic, power, frequency, and intention is still on your side. You can try again and add more energy in the direction of your desired outcome by casting another spell.

Give it some deep thought. What else is at play? Did you really take inspired action? Are you totally honest with yourself about what you want? Are there any thoughts or feelings about your spell that feel "off"? Are you grateful for what you already have? Can you "give back" or reciprocate with service or energy?

FOR MORE TIPS AND INSPIRATION:

Seek out websites, books, podcasts, and videos on spirituality. Follow your intuition and curiosity to deepen your practice and find your own style. And check out other books in the *Coloring Book of Shadows* series, like the *Book of Spells* and *Witch Life*.

SOUTHERN HEMISPHERE MAGIC

If you're in the Southern Hemisphere in a place like Australia, there are a couple of differences that you'll need to note.

The biggest difference is that since seasonal shifts are opposite on the calendar year, you'll feel the energy of Samhain around May 1 instead of October 31.

Southern Hemisphere "spinning and circle casting" will go "sun wise" according to the south—counterclockwise for invoking (drawing in), clockwise for banishing (letting go).

North and South Elements are also typically swapped in Southern Hemisphere magic—North = Fire, South = Earth.

So Mote it Be.

Jessica Elliott
Color Assistant

Bollank
Color & Art Assistant

Fiona Horne
Editor of Magick
& Editor
FionaHorne.com

Wendy Ledger
Editor
WendyLedgerAuthor.com

Kae-Marie
Denino Editor

THANK YOU!

About the Artist

Amy Cesari
(and her familiar, Cornelius)

Amy is an author and illustrator who loves animated musicals. She also likes watercolor painting, witchcraft, and walking on the beach in a really big sun hat.

Not only does she own every Nintendo game console ever made, she's earned several fancy diplomas and enjoys continued studies in various magical practices.

CONTACT AMY AND SEE MORE BOOKS, PRINTABLE PAGES, AND ART:

Amy@ColoringBookofShadows.com
ColoringBookofShadows.com

Made in the USA
Las Vegas, NV
17 May 2024

90028716R00085